TREES
OF THE WORLD

DAVID LAMBERT

The Bookwright Press
New York · 1986

Topics

All the words that appear
in **bold** are explained in the
glossary on page 30.

First published in the United States in 1986 by
The Bookwright Press
387 Park Avenue South
New York, NY 10016

First published in 1985 by
Wayland (Publishers) Ltd
61 Western Road, Hove
East Sussex BN3 1JD, England

© Copyright 1985 Wayland (Publishers) Ltd

ISBN 0–531–18086–7
Library of Congress Catalog Card Number: 86:–70183

Phototypeset by
Kalligraphics Ltd, Redhill, Surrey
Printed in Italy by
G. Canale & C.S.p.A., Turin

Contents

Food Factories

If you cut open a ripe acorn, inside its rainproof coat you will find a root, a shoot, and two small leaves. An acorn is no bigger than the top of someone's thumb, but it has everything it needs to grow into a mighty tree.

Trees include the biggest living things on Earth. Some grow up to 100 meters (330 feet) tall; others, however, grow no taller than grass. But whatever their size, all trees are made in the same way. Each one has three main parts: **roots**, **trunk** and **crown**. These parts work together, the way machines inside a factory work together, to produce food.

Oak trees grow from tiny acorns like these.

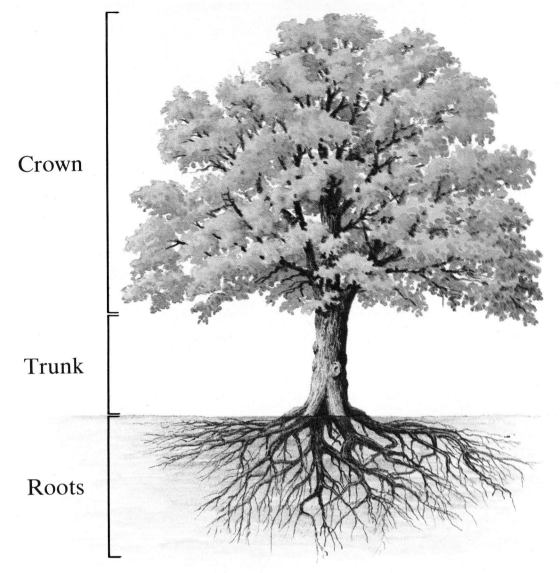

Crown

Trunk

Roots

The parts of a tree.

Roots spread down and out through soil. They hold a tree firmly in the ground and help to keep its trunk upright. They also take in water and **minerals** from the soil. Near each root tip is a brush of tiny root hairs. These cling to particles of soil and soak up water. This water is pulled up through the trunk

5

Roots spread out through the soil to collect water and minerals.

to replace the **water vapor** that escapes from the leaves into the air.

The trunk holds the crown high above the ground to give it light and air. By looking at a tree stump you can see how a tree trunk works. An outer skin of **bark** protects the inside of the trunk from disease and damage. Just beneath the bark most trees have a ring of growing **cells**, called the **cambium**. The cells of this ring form tiny tubes that carry food down from the leaves to the roots. Inside the cambium is the wood of the tree trunk. Wood makes the tree trunk strong enough to bear the weight of all the branches, twigs and leaves. Tiny tubes in wood carry water and minerals up from the roots.

Each year the trunk gets thicker as one new **growth ring** is produced. If you count the growth rings on a tree stump you can find out how old the tree was when it was cut down.

The branches, twigs and leaves of a tree form the crown. Leaves open up from buds that grow on twigs. Each leaf has special cells containing the green chemical, **chlorophyll**. Chlorophyll uses the energy in sunlight to turn water and carbon dioxide gas into food for the tree.

A cross section of a tree trunk.

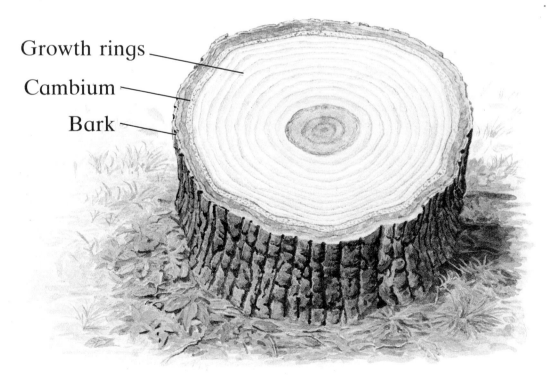

Growth rings

Cambium

Bark

Kinds of Trees

There are two main kinds of trees. One type produces seeds that have no outer covering, whereas the seeds of the other type are surrounded by a seed case called a fruit.

Most trees with unprotected seeds have leaves that look like little needles. Firs, larches, pines and spruces are all needle-leaved trees. You can often tell which tree is which by looking at their leaves. For instance, fir and spruce leaves grow all along the twigs. Pine leaves grow in clusters of two to five. Larch leaves grow in clusters of ten to thirty.

All needle-leaved trees are called **conifers**, or cone-bearers, and most of them are evergreen,

The needle-shaped leaves of this spruce grow all along the twigs.

This monkey puzzle tree has broad leaves, even though it is a conifer.

which means they keep their leaves throughout the year. Their seeds grow inside a **cone**, which opens up when the seeds are ripe and lets them fall. Many conifer seeds have little wings that help the wind to scatter them before they land, so that when the seeds sprout, they are not overcrowded.

Not every conifer has narrow leaves. The Chilean monkey puzzle and the kauri pine are broad-leaved trees, but they also produce cones.

Conifers are able to flourish in harsh conditions. Their tough, narrow leaves endure both cold and drought. Umbrella pines thrive in the dry, sandy soils around the Mediterranean Sea. Conifers with pointed crowns are able to survive long, cold, snowy winters. Huge forests of needle-leaved conifers form a band that runs throughout the northern regions of the world. Snow slips easily off their pointed tops and does not break their springy branches. Forests of conifers have also taken root on the steep slopes of mountain ranges, like the North American Rockies and Asia's Himalayas.

Conifers can survive extreme cold.

Different regions of the world are home to some unusual conifers. The largest living things in the world are the giant sequoia trees that grow in parts of California. One conifer, which has been named the General Sherman tree, in the Sequoia National Park in California soars 83 meters (272 feet) above the ground and weighs more than 6,600 tons. Some of the oldest trees on earth are the small, twisted bristlecone pines of the southwestern United States. One lived for 4,900 years before it was cut down. Cedars found in Japan and eastern China may be even older.

The trunk of a giant sequoia tree.

Most trees with broad, flat leaves are **flowering plants**, with seeds protected by a fruit. Broad-leaved trees like elms, oaks and beeches grow well in much of Europe, Asia and North America. They are mostly **deciduous**: they lose all their leaves in winter. The leaves turn yellow, brown or red before dying and falling from the tree. In this way, trees with tender leaves protect themselves from damage at the coldest, windiest time of year.

Deciduous broad-leaved trees also grow in hot lands with a long dry season. The leaves fall before the drought begins and this stops the trees from losing too much precious moisture.

Each spring, deciduous trees put out new leaves from buds like these.

The drip tip of a tropical leaf.

There are some broad-leaved trees that are evergreen. For instance, holly keeps its tough, shiny leaves all year long, and in the hot rain forests of South America, Africa and Southeast Asia most trees are broad-leaved evergreens. These trees don't ever shed all their leaves at once because the weather there is always warm and wet. Many leaves even have a long, pointed "drip tip" to let raindrops run off more easily. Many rain forest trees have mighty trunks propped up by buttress roots that look like massive planks.

Although no broad-leaved trees grow as old or as large as some conifers, they can be just as unusual. The baobab of Africa has a fat trunk that can be twice as far around as it is high. The banyan tree is a fig tree with roots that grow down from its many branches. Because these roots appear very similar to the trunk of the tree, a big banyan can look

A banyan tree in Mauritius.

Coconut palms are often found close to the sea-shore.

like a whole grove of trees. Coconut palms are unusual for the way they spread. Ripe coconuts fall into the sea and float for many miles before the waves wash them ashore. The nuts then take root and sprout. In this way coconut palms have spread to lands all around the warm oceans of the world.

15

Useful Trees

Trees help wild plants, wild animals and people in all sorts of ways.

Woodland trees give smaller plants shade, shelter and support. The trees' spreading branches keep the woodland floor damp and shady. Ferns and mosses, which grow best in cool, wet places, benefit from the shelter the trees give them. Trees also provide a surface on which small plants can grow. In mild climates tiny plants called algae attach themselves to tree trunks and color them green.

Climbing plants, like ivy and lianas, grow high above the ground by clinging to tree trunks. In

Sheltered by trees, small plants and shrubs thrive on the forest floor.

places where the air is always damp, plants such as ferns and bromeliads even sprout on branches. They push their roots into crevices in tree branches where rotting leaves and rainwater have collected. Ferns and bromeliads make their own food, but mistletoe sucks some nourishment from the trees on which it grows. Plants such as mistletoe are called **parasites**.

Trees produce food for themselves, but when they die they in turn become food for plantlike growths called **fungi**. Dead branches and leaves also nourish soil, thus helping other trees and plants to grow.

Fungi growing on a tree trunk.

These langurs are able to find food and safety in the treetops.

Trees also help wild creatures. Climbing and flying animals are at home among the branches. Up there, well above the forest floor, birds, squirrels and monkeys are safe from enemies that cannot climb. They are able to move about in the treetops and seldom need to come down to the ground. Birds simply fly from tree to tree, squirrels leap from branch to branch and monkeys run along branches on all fours. Gibbons, which are a type of ape, swing along, hanging by their arms.

Creatures of many kinds actually make their homes high up in trees. Chimpanzees sleep on nests of leafy twigs, and most birds lay their eggs in treetop nests. Woodpeckers raise their families in hollow tree trunks. Tailorbirds and weaver ants fasten leaves together to make their fragile homes.

Some animals that live on the ground use trees to build their homes. Beavers gnaw through small trees to cut them down. Then they pile the trees in pools to build their homes, which are called lodges.

A beaver lodge in North America.

When food is scarce, deer will chew tree bark.

Animals large and small find food among the trees. Hungry deer and rabbits gnaw bark. Squirrels nibble buds and nuts. Beetle grubs feed on dead wood. Caterpillars eat leaves. Many beetles and caterpillars form food for larger creatures: woodpeckers peck through wood to capture beetle grubs and tits and warblers feast on caterpillars. There are, however, even bigger hunters among the trees. Hawks swoop down and kill unsuspecting small birds and the harpy eagle of South America feeds on monkeys and other mammals.

People, too, benefit from the food provided by trees. From orchard trees come tasty fruits including apples, peaches, pears and oranges. Cocoa and coffee are made with seeds from trees that grow in hot countries. Much of the world's cooking oil comes from the fruits of olive trees and oil palms.

Harvesting oranges in South Africa.

Trees help people in more ways than you might suppose. Many useful objects in our homes and yards come from trees. Wooden chairs and tables are made of strong lumber from such **hardwood trees** as beech, oak, mahogany and teak. Most wood that we use, however, comes from **softwood trees** like pines and firs. These conifers provide beams and planks for roofs and floors. Each day, factory machines turn huge amounts of softwood into wood pulp for making paper.

Almost any part of a tree can be put to some use. Palm leaves roof huts in hot countries. Truck and car tires are often made from the milky juice that is

These women are stacking sheets of paper made from mulberry wood.

"tapped" from the trunks of rubber trees and then hardened into rubber.

Perhaps the best thing about trees is that they are there at all. Tree roots soak up rainwater like sponges and hold the soil together. On steep slopes this stops rainwater from washing the soil away. What is more, tree leaves give off water vapor into the air. This moistens air and helps to produce enough rain for crops to grow.

Rubber-tapping in Malaysia.

Enemies and Friends

Like all things in nature, trees have both enemies and friends.

Most trees' worst enemies are pests and diseases. These can enter trees through wounds in the bark where branches have been snapped by gales or chewed by animals. For example, elm bark beetles pick up a tiny fungus on their feet which causes Dutch elm disease. When the beetles feed on twigs, the fungus gets inside the tree and kills it. Dutch elm disease has destroyed millions of elm trees in North America and Europe.

These trees have been killed by Dutch elm disease.

Most trees, in fact, can be attacked by pests and diseases, but luckily, the bark usually keeps them from getting inside the tree and causing serious damage. Many injured trees are also able to seal off a damaged part with sticky substances to keep diseases from entering the tree.

Birds help trees to survive by eating insects that could spread disease, and insects themselves are sometimes used by farmers to eat other insects. In California, orange growers once let loose millions of

Birds like this owl help trees by eating caterpillars and other insects.

A plane tree in a park in London, England.

Australian chalcid wasps. The wasps ate the mealybugs that had been damaging the farmers' orange trees. Each year, most farmers spray their orchards with chemicals, to kill off plant and insect pests before they start to do much damage.

Smoke is an enemy of most trees. They cannot stand the sooty, smoky atmospheres some cities have. Plane trees are an exception and they grew well even in the heart of London, England when it was one of the dirtiest, sootiest cities in the world.

Fire is much more dangerous than smoke. Forest fires have destroyed millions of trees. Yet some species can endure the flames. Baobabs have thick bark that protects the living tissue from the heat. Where fires are frequent, some trees survive by extending underground suckers into the cool earth below the fire. North America's jack pine actually needs the heat from forest fires to open its pine cones and free the seeds inside. Without forest fires, the seeds could not drop and sprout.

A forest fire in Australia.

The worst enemies of millions of forest trees are people. All around the world trees are being felled, as people clear forests to make space for new farms or to use their trees as lumber. When trees are destroyed, their roots no longer guard the soil against the effects of rainwater. On steep hills rain washes all the soil away and plants are unable to grow. Forests used to cover vast areas of countries such as the Caribbean island nation of Haiti, but now most of the trees have gone. Soon Haiti could

Each year, vast areas of the world's forests are destroyed.

become a desert.

While some people clear away whole forests, however, others work hard to save them. In many lands, the **United Nations Food and Agriculture Organization** teaches people why and how they should plant new trees. Now, in many of the forests of Europe and North America, foresters cut down only small patches at a time. Then they plant seedlings on the land they have cleared so that young trees are always growing up to replace the old ones that have gone.

Young trees being grown in a nursery in Denmark.

Glossary

Bark The tough, corky skin that covers tree trunks, branches and twigs.

Cambium A ring of growing cells just inside the bark of most kinds of trees.

Cells The tiny building blocks that trees and all other living things are made of. Even small trees have millions of cells.

Chlorophyll The substance that makes leaves green. Chlorophyll uses water, carbon dioxide and the Sun's energy to produce sugar. This sugar provides food for trees.

Cone A mass of wooden scales bearing conifer seeds.

Conifers Trees that produce their seeds in cones.

Crown The branches, twigs and leaves of a tree.

Deciduous Deciduous trees shed all their leaves once a year.

Flowering plants Plants that produce seeds surrounded by a seed case called a fruit.

Fungi (*singular*: fungus) Plantlike living things that have no chlorophyll. Some grow as big as a football, others are too tiny to be seen without a microscope.

Growth ring A ring of new cells formed inside a tree each year.

Hardwood trees Broad-leaved flowering trees. The wood of some hardwood trees is in fact very soft.

Minerals Chemicals that tree roots take from the soil to help the tree grow.

Parasites Animals or plants that live and feed on others.

Roots Roots grow underground. They spread out to support the tree's trunk and crown. Roots also take in minerals and water.

Softwood trees Firs, pines, spruces and other conifers. Some softwood trees have harder wood than many hardwoods.

Trunk The woody stem of a tree. Tubes inside the trunk take food down from the leaves to the roots. Other tubes carry water and minerals from the roots to the leaves.

United Nations Food and Agriculture Organization This organization tries to make the world's people better fed. Its workers teach people in many lands how to grow crops, catch fish and care for trees.

Water vapor Tiny, invisible particles of water in the air. Minute holes in leaves allow water vapor to escape into the air.

Books to Read

Brown, Anne E. *Monarchs of the Forest: The Story of the Redwoods.* New York: Dodd, Mead, 1984.

Dickinson, Jane. *All About Trees.* Mahwah, NJ: Troll Associates, 1983.

Dowden, Anne O. *The Blossom on the Bough: A Book of Trees.* New York: Crowell Junior Books, 1985.

List, Albert. *A Walk in the Forest: The Woodlands of North America.* New York: Crowell Junior Books, 1977.

Sabin, Francene. *Wonders of the Forest.* Mahwah, NJ: Troll Associates, 1979.

Selsam, Millicent. *Tree Flowers.* New York: Morrow, 1984.

Whipple, Jane B. *Forest Resources.* New York: Franklin Watts, 1985.

Acknowledgments

The illustrations in this book were provided by: Camerapix Hutchison Library 19, 20, 22; Bruce Coleman Ltd 4 (Jane Burton), 6 (Philip H. Evans), 8 (John Shaw), 9 (Francisco Erize), 12 and 26 (Eric Crichton), 13 (Waina Cheng), 17 (Geoff, Doré), 18 (Gunter Ziesler), 25 (Roger Wilmshurst), 27 (Fritz Prenzel); Geoscience Features 10, 11, 16; Cliff Meadway 5, 7; NHPA 23 (Douglas Dickins), 24 (E. A. James); Seaphot Limited 14 (Ivor Edmunds), 28 (Richard Matthews); Wayland Picture Library 15, 21, 29; ZEFA *front cover.*

Index